SARASWATI
(GĀYATRI, SAVITRI, BAG DEVI)

by
Chitralekha Singh
Prrem Nath

CREST PUBLISHING HOUSE
(A JAICO ENTERPRISE)
G-2, 16 Ansari Road, Daryaganj
New Delhi - 110002

© Crest Publishing House

No part of this book may be reproduced or utilized in any form or by any means, electronics or meachanical including photocopying, recording or by any information storage and retrievel system, without permission in writing from the publishers.

SARASWATI
ISBN 81-242-0155-2

First Edition : 1999

Published by :
CREST PUBLISHING HOUSE
(A Jaico Enterprise)
G-2, 16, Ansari Road, Darya Ganj,
New Delhi-110002.

Printed by :
Efficient Offset Printers
215, Shahzada Bagh Industrial Complex
Phase II, Delhi-110035

Contents

PREFACE	IV
Chapters	**Page No.**
I. INTRODUCTION	1
II. SARASWATI: THE ORIGIN	7
III. SARASWATI: THE GODDESS	11
IV. THE RIVER SARASWATI	25
V. KURUKSHETRA	33
VI. TRIPLE DIVINITIES AND SUN GOD	43
VII. DYNAMIC FORM OF SOUND	57
VIII. MAHĀ SARASWATI	61
IX. WORSHIP AND PRAYERS	63
X. FESTIVALS AND FAIRS	69
XI. LEARNING AND LITERATURE	73
XII. PILGRIMAGE, TEMPLES AND SHRINES	77
XIII. ICONOGRAPHY, SCULPTURE AND PAINTINGS	83

Preface

'Hinduism is as broad as the universe' (Gandhi). Religion has its influence in every country, it is more so in India. 'Take away religion from India, nothing would be left' (Vivekananda). Every system of Indian philosophic though gives us a practical way of reaching the supreme ideal. Everything there related to this discipline (way) is called a YOGA such as Jñāna yoga or the way of knowledge, Bhakti yoga or the way of devotion and KARMA yoga or the way of action viz theoretical,emotional and practical aspects. Knowledge and action should go together, as is the teaching in SRIMAD BHAGWAT GITA. Knowledge, the object of knowledge and the knowing subjects are the threefold incitement to action; the instrument, the action and the agent, the threefold components of action.

Intelligence, wisdom and learning are essential for the performance of all actions (Karma) and it is the awarding of these three components of Jñāna (knowledge) that the boons of Goddess Saraswati play an important role in the wordly life. Goddess Saraswati, related to SAVITRI (Sun) is one of the trinity, the others being Gāyatri, and Savitri or the Bāg (Vāk) devi of the Vedas. Saraswati is the Goddess of learning, intelligence, wisdom and the consort of B'rhma, the creator.

As is the case with B'rhma, on whom the published literature and also worship is less, so is the case with Saraswati. Though she is the Goddess of knowledge, yet the writers have not done justice to their Goddess. Even in devotion, the temples, shrines and pilgrimage places of this Goddess, are few and far between.

In this small book, which is meant to enlighten the readers about this important Goddess, an attempt has been made to give a wide description of the Goddess in all different aspects, as a river, river Goddess, a Puranic (postvedic) Goddess and in her manifestations as Gāyatri, Savitri and Bāg (Vāk) devi. Different versions of her origin, pilgrimage places and Kurukshetra of (MAHĀBHĀRATA) have been described in some greater details.

The description in the book is based on the sacred scriptures, epics and the Puranas and is authenticated.

This small book, its reading and the performance of the worship ritual in it will not only, be of interest to the readers, but also will bring blessings of the Goddess, if adopted in daily practice. Iconographers, artists will find some points of interest in the book. Pilgrims will be greatly benefitted by the study of the book.

We have made great efforts to collect and present all about the Goddess. The authors will be obliged to know its shortcomings from the readers.

We are obliged to Shri S.C. Sethi executive manager, Jaico enterprise for his all time encouragement and suggestions.

We are thankful to CREST PUBLISHING HOUSE for the illustrious publication of the book, in its beauty.

CHITRANGAN   CHITRALEKHA
KRISHNAPURI   PRREM NATH
AGRA 282 001

CHAPTER I
INTRODUCTION

In the origin and development of the creation, divine power ŚAKTI has an important place. Śakti being of voluntarily controlled nature, has been accepted in female form. Hence in the creation, the female has the highest place. She is available to humanity for creation and nourishment in the form of Abhey (Fearlessness) boon. From the most ancient scripture R'gveda of the Vedic period, one gains knowledge about Śakti. At that time among Vedic deities PRITHVI (Earth) or nature, in the form of the mother was worshipped.

The Vedic deities of The R'gvedic period do not have a heirarchy of rank. Each hymn in Vedas extols a particular God and pays him the highest tribute, in his ecstasy the poet regards that God as the greatest, but in another hymn, another God is similarly extolled. A convenient classification of R'gvedic deities is:-

(a) CELESTIAL:- Surya (Sun); Ushas (Dawn); Asvins (Stars); Savitri (Bāg Devi).

(b) ATMOSPHERIC:- Indra (storm); Vayu (Wind); Varuna (Sky); Parjanaya (Rain-Cloud); Rudra (Destroyer).

(c) Terrestrial:- Agne (Fire); Soma (Plant); Saraswati (River) Prithvi (Earth).

The protecting power of VIŚNU has eight aspects and each of them is pictured as a GODDESS:-

1. SRIDEVI, the goddess of wealth and fortune.
2. BHŪDEVI, representing the earth and often like SriDevi, as the junior consort of Viṡnu, stands for sovereignity over the earth.
3. SARASWATI signifies learning.
4. PRITI is love personified.
5. KRITI
6. SĀNTI } give fame and peace.
7. TUSTI
8. PUṠTI } grant pleasure and strength.

The classical myths of DEVI are numerous and divergent. As SARASWATI, she is the Goddess of learning, In the VEDAS, Saraswati was a water deity, Goddess of the river Saraswati, which was to the early Hindus as worshipfull, as Ganges is to their descendents now. The next stage in her mythological history was her identification with the holy rituals performed on her banks, influencing the composition of hymns and thus identified with VĀCH, the Goddess of speech. Later myths diminish Saraswati's power and she was said to be identified with VIRĀJ, the female half of Purusha or Prajapati and thus an instrument of creation. Most generally she is considered to be the creature and consort of B'rhma and is called the Mother of the VEDAS, executing what B'rhma conceived with his creative intelligence. She is the Sakti, the power and consort of creator B'rhma, so she is the procreatrix, the mother of the entire creation. In symbology, she represents the power and intelligence of B'rhma, without which organised creation is impossible. To show that this intelligent power is stupendous and absolutely pure, She is pictured as white

INTRODUCTION

and dazzling. The four arms show her unimpeded power in all four directions or her all pervasiveness.

Some of the other names of Goddess Saraswati are Satarupa, Sāvitri, Vāch Gāyatri and Brahami; as also Bāg Devi, Brahamani and BHĀRATI, who in ancient times, on the ninth day of winter, was invoked by the Gods in a prayer:-

> 'O fair complexioned, whose supreme attribute is the essence of B'rhm knowledge, one who holds a Veena and a book, one who awards fearlessness and destroys the gloom of ignorance, who holds a garland of quartz, who is seated on a lotus throne, I pray to that Parmeshwari Bhagvati, knowledge giver SĀRDĀ.

When the epic era began, the centre of Aryan civilisation was in the valleys of the Ganges and the Yamuna, where rose flourishing kingdoms of the Kurus, the Panchālās, the Sālvas and the Matsyas, as well as the powerful confederacy of the Yadavās of Mathura. Large tracts even in this region were still covered with forests, some of which, notably the Khāndavavana, the Kāmyaka Vana and the Dvaitavana find prominent mention in the epic narrative. Through these and other woodlands glided several streams like the Saraswati, the Drishādvati and the Mālini, the banks of which were dotted over with serene hermitages of the seers and the sages, 'echoing with some sweet songs of birds and clad with flowery attire of many colours'. The people of the holy land watered by the Saraswati and the Yamuna looked askance at the new type of imperialism that had been evolved on the banks of the Sone.

King Yayati, in the epic period, was the sixth descendent from Daksheye (created from the right thumb of B'rhma), who had five sons from his two wives named

Dayeyāni and Sarmishta. From Devayani's younger son Yadu developed the Yadavas. From Sarmishta's son PURU developed Bharat and through Shantanu and Vichitraveerya's consort Ambikā-came Dhritrāshtra (Kauravas) and from the other wife Ambalika came Pāndu and the Pandavas of the Mahābhārata. Yayati was a very pious and religious king and it is said that Saraswati granted milk ghee to his realm. Yayati performed many sacrifices (Yageyas) and worshipped Gods and ancestors with devotion and looked after his subjects with love. He married Devyāni, daughter of saint Shukracharay and Sarmishta, a servant maid. By cures of Shukracharaye, Yayati became old in young age. On this request he was given a boon that if anyone adopted his old age, he could still live as a young man and enjoy youth. All the sons were given the choice one after the other, but all refused, except PURU, who agreed. Yayati enjoyed youth for a thousand years and then giving up the kingship to PURU, went into the forests, undertaking asceticism, eating only fruits and forest products, still later only the wind, later standing on one leg, he undertook severe asceticism and mediation, till he gave up his life. All this happened on the banks of the Saraswati, the most sacred river of the times and revered by the Gods. Puru was the ancestor of the EPIC Aryans.

Archaeologists have recently unearthed a 5000 years old wooden board, which shows Indus Saraswati Script. New research has shown that nearly two thirds of Indus civilisation sites were on the Saraswati river, only five percent on Indus river and the rest in Gujarat, and Uttar Pradesh, south and east of the Saraswati. This script (Indus Saraswati) became rare after 2000 BC, possibly due to drying up of Saraswati around the epic period of

INTRODUCTION

Mahābhārata. Indus civilisation, generally known sofar, has been renamed INDUS SARASWATI CIVILISATION.

Literally Saraswati means 'the flowing one'. In the R'gveda, she represents a river with the presiding deity over it. Hence she is connected with fertility and purification. Some of the names by which Saraswati is described are SĀRADĀ viz giver of essence; VĀGISVARI viz: Mistress of speech; BRĀHMI viz wife of B'rhma' MAHĀVIDYĀ signifying supreme knowledge and so on. These names describing her in the VEDAS as a river, were later on developed in mythology as Goddess representing power and intelligence from which organised creation proceeds. The flowing one can represent speech allegorically and perfect speech presupposes power and intelligence.

R'g VEDA (1 : 3 : 10 -12) praises BĀG DEVI SARASWATI. She has been applauded for giving food, successful completion of yageye, as the encouragement for TRUTH, the giver of higher wisdom and the ONE who enlightens with the vast sea of knowledge. She is the inspiration for intelligence and good deeds. She has two forms:- One river form and the other divine.

In R'g VEDA (10 : 125) BagDevi has been called as wielding eleven Rudras, eight Vasus, twelve Aditeyas, Visva Devi, Mitra and Varuna, as well Agni. Saraswati declares that she is the nourisher of Soma, Twasta, Pusha and Bhāgdeva. To end Trilok, she supports Visnu, B'rhma and Prajāpati. She is ISVARI of the whole universe and the giver of wealth to the devotees and that they acquire fortune and prosperity from HER.

To the one, on whom she (Bāgdevi : Saraswati) is pleased, she makes him radical tempered, enlightened, melodious, comparable to B'rhma and that she also supports Prithvi (Earth).

SARASWATI

Saraswati, Consort of Brahma

CHAPTER II

SARASWATI: THE ORIGIN

Saraswati, as a river Goddess in the Vedas, and as a Goddess in later mythology, has many versions about her origin.

B'rhma, the creator, and Saraswati, his consort, are the subject of several tales in Hindu mythological literature:-

1. B'rhma was born out of the golden egg, produced in the boundless causal waters. Has consort VĀC (SARASWATI) was manifested out of Him. From their union were born all the creatures of the world.

2. B'rhma represents the VEDĀS, and Saraswati their spirit and meaning. Hence all knowledge, sacred and secular, has precedence from them.

3. HAYAGRIVA is the God of learning, a kin to the Goddess Saraswati.

The origin of Goddess Saraswati is attributable to a conference between B'rhmā, Viṣnu and Śiva, to decide the punishment to be given to Andhaka (son of Kashyap), who had attempted to steal away the sacred Parijata tree from the Swarg (Heaven). When the trinity looked at one another, their combined energy formed a red, white and black brilliantly illuminated feminine form. This divine creation further divided into three and the white one

SARASWATI

SARASWATI - (SOUTH INDIA)

SARASWATI: THE ORIGIN

became Goddess Saraswati which represented the past; a part of the trio of Goddesses 'Saraswati Laksmi and Parvati).

In another version, B'rhmā created Saraswati out of his own substance. She was so beautiful that B'rhmā was so enamoured by her beauty, that he acquired three more heads to look at Saraswati in the directions, in which she went. Finally when she flew to the skies, B'rhmā acquired fifth head to look upwards at her. She was also called Satārupā, Sāvitri, Vāc, Gāyatri and Brahamāni.

In VAMANĀ PURANĀ Chapter 32, her origin is explained by Mahrishi Lom Harsha that Saraswati had its source in a Palaksa tree and was taken out by prayers and invokation. She is held as most sacred of all rivers.

The Indian concept of a river is that of a sustaining mother, a fertility Goddess and both a physical and a spiritual cleanser. Respect for the river Goddesses was deeply rooted among the people of the Vedic age. Numerous hymns to Saraswati (Bāg Devi, Vāc) are to be found in the R'GVEDA; however no specific mention of other rivers, deified in later periods, occur in this text. Rather the rivers are addressed as a composite group 'O Ye water' (R'gVeda 10.75). In this long hymn to Saraswati, it is stated that she descended from the sky, which is perhaps, an early anticipation of the birth of Ganga.

After the DHARAM STOTRA, from the left side of B'rhma, a girl appeared. That idol like was second Kamalalaya (Laxmi) in appearence. After that from his mouth, fair complexioned, holding a Veena and a book in her hands, Goddess emerged. She had the glitter of crores of full moons. Her eyes were like scattered lotus flowers in winter.

She was clad in pure white garments, matching with her body, and was adorned with be jewelled ornaments. Her beautiful teeth were closely erupted and she was most beautiful among all beauties. She was the most honoured in the hymns and was the producer of scholars of Shāstras, sacred scriptures. she was the worshipped Goddess of speech and revered Goddess of the poets, scholars and the musicians. She was Saraswati, a Goddess full of pious element calm and subtle in form, blissful and compassionate. At her very emergence, she sang a song in front of Govind; a song which personified her name and qualities. After that she performed a dance. then Saraswati worshipped Viṣnu (Hari) and praised with folded hands, all deeds of Viṣnu, that he had performed through the ages.

'I pray to the one, located in the Rās mandal and those interested in delight, installed on a be jewelled throne, I pay my respects to the Lord of Rāsa (Sri K'rsna) and those who enjoy Rāsa.' After paying reverence to the one, who performed Rāsa.' with Gopis, she sat on the throne. This is a hymn to Saraswati. The one, who recites this hymn in the morning, becomes intelligent, prosperous, knowledgeable and always bears sons. (Braham Veyvaratey Puranā Mrishti Nirupan part 54-59).

Saraswati, as a supreme Goddess, is all important and her attributes are numerous.

CHAPTER III

SARASWATI: THE GODDESS

Saraswati as a, Goddess was highly respected by other deities. In the Vedic ritual, AGNI occupied the most important position. He carried the oblations to Gods in heaven and also brought the Gods to the sacrificial around on earth. In this context R'GVEDA V S 8 states :-

'Ila, Saraswati, Māhi, three Goddesses.

Who bring as weal,

Be seated harmless on the grass'.

The classical myths of Devi are numerous and divergent. As Sarasati, she is the Goddess of learning, wife of B'rhma in the later mythology and personified in the river Saraswati. River Saraswati, the ancient India, was to the early Hindus, what the Ganges is to their descendents today. River Saraswati has been frequently mentioned in R'GVEDA (II.41.16.9) and has been termed 'NADITAMA'. A poetic version is:-

'Best mother, best of rivers, best of Goddesses Saraswati,

We are, as it were of no repute,

Dear mother, give us thou renown.

GANEŚA is usually described as the God of learning

SARASWATI

SARASWATI
(FOLK-LORE)

SARASWATI: THE GODDESS

and patron of letters, whereas the whole province of speech, Language of literature, is really placed under the realm of Saraswati. Thus the first verse of MAHĀBHĀRATA epic pays homage to Saraswati, not to Ganesa.

RGVEDA (II.4.9.17)

'In thee, Saraswati, who are divine,

All existences are assembled in, thee,

Rejoice Goddess, among the shunahotras (Hymns),

Grant us, O'Goddess, progeny'.

In another hymn (R'GVEDA II.4.9.18):-

'Saraswati, abounding in food, abounding in water,

Be propitiated by these oblations,

which the grit samadas offer,

As acceptable to thee, and precious to Gods'.

RGVEDA (II.3.9.8) in appellation:-

'Saraswati, do thou protect us, associated with the Maruts and firm (of purpose), overcome our foes, whilst Indra slays the Chief of Shandikas, defying him and confiding in his strength.

R'GVEDA (I.24.9.8) in prayer:-

BHĀRATI (the Goddess presiding heaven), ILA (over the earth), Saraswati (over the firmament), I invoke you all, That you may direct us to prosperity'.

R'GVEDA (3.12) applauds Saraswati:-

'Saraswati produces a vast sea. She encourages the senses to gain knowledge'.

Markandeye in VAMANA PURANA addressing Saraswati says:- 'O' Devi, your magnificent form is beyond my description and none else can describe it, because no tongue, larynx or lips, can describe it, That is B'rhmā, Visnu, Siva, Chandrama (Moon) and Surya (SUN) and the light, the basis of home of the world, the form of the universe the Soulx of the Universe is Māheswar. The principle of Sankheye care Vedic and have been incorporated in many branches. that is eternal, central and in deep rooted form. That is always the truth and the Untruth. that one exists in many forms and is a mixture of thoughts and differences. That is indescribable, alomorphic, amphibiological and the refuge for three GUNAS (Sattva, Rajas, and Tamas). It has been learnt from many different powers and is a division of many powers. The SANKHEYS and MAHASANKHEYS of comfort elements are virtuous. O'Devi, you have pervaded this universe, in such a way, that B'rhma, who lives in Advait conditions, has been permeated in DVAITA.'

'Those, who are wealthy and those who are not, others who ar stationary and are miserable, subtle, who are on the earth or in the cosmos or at any-other place, You are the one who enlightens them, gives them direction. Those, who are extinct and corporeal in unity and if there is some deed in the spirits or if there is anything in the Gods, may be in writing or have any relation to words and vowels, all those are your forms'.

As mentioned in R'GVEDA (VI.61.1) DIVODASA, was born to Vadhryāsava, by the blessings of the Goddess

Saraswati, which is interpreted as him having been born on the banks of the river Saraswati. Divodāsa's main exploit was his victory over SAMBARA. Sambarā's territory was in the punjab hills. The scene of the battle MAHĀBHĀRĀTA, is located in the Kangra hills of the Himalāyās, on the ground that the BHARATĀS were in occupation of the nearby lands round about the river Saraswati and PARUSNI (RAVI). Sanvarna invaded Hastinapur from western side of the Indus and defeated Bharatās and his son KURU and Kurus of Kurukshetra, went south east through Bactriana and Hindukush, moved into Punjab and occupied Saraswati Yamuna region.

The descendents of MANU in Brahamvarta (Foot of Himalyas) established Vidhan, Kosala and Vaisali realms. Videgha Mathava accompanied by his priest GOTAMA carried the sacred fire from the banks of river Saraswati, to the banks of the river Sadanira (modern Gandaki) and established himself as the first ruler of the Vedehan Kingdom.

'SARASWATI is the Hindu minerva, the Goddess of learning and of speech. She invented Sanskrit and is the St Luke of the East, as she is patroness of the arts and sciences.

Saraswati is the goddess of all the creative arts, and in particular of poetry and music, learning and science. Her original name is SWARASWATI and Saraswati is an oral deformation. Swar means sound, voice, tone or a note. Swaras are find sentiment. R'GVEDA (1.3.10) describes Saraswati, as the Goddess of speech. By imparting the rhythm of words, She blesses us with pleasent happy behaviour. Hymn 11 of the same:- 'Saraswati inculcates true speech and is a cause for unity. She has been blessed by all sacred fires (Yageyas). Hymn 12 of the same symbolises Saraswati as the source of enlightenment of words (speech). She appears as a source for all in the form of SOUL.

- Saraswati is the Goddess of the treasure of sound. She blesses us with words and through that good behaviour. By her thought, the words flow in showers. May she accept our yagey (Sacrifice).

Goddess Saraswati instigates (encourages) true speech and is the one who advises good actions/wisdom. Saraswati accepts our yageyas.

- Saraswati, by her directions, makes great words and awakens the people. She appears as the soul of all sources.

'O' merciful Goddess Saraswati. May you become the bestower of comfort and welfare for us all. We should not be debarred from your appearence. 'O' mother Saraswati, may you feed us with your nourishing, comfort giving, wealth increasing milk. This sweet milk fulfills all our desires'.

Seeking the blessings of all other Gods, the devotees first pray to Saraswati to obtain initial power (Sakti). Whenever, a yegeya has to be in actions, have been invokving Saraswati, as the invigorator of good behaviour, since that Vedic era. Those who conscientiously pray to Saraswati, the Goddess blesses them with the wishfull boons. A devotee prays: 'Since I have been wandering hither and thither for the fulfilment of my desires, which I expressed before many and the worries and the suffering that I have undergone through, which injured my inner soul and conscience, I pray to Goddess Saraswati that she may give me a boon to heal those injuries by her mercy'.

FORM AND ATTRIBUTES

Post Vedic Saraswati, according to her internal attributes, attained her outer form. Who is fair, because she is the giver of knowledge. remover of ignorance (darkness), bestower of subtlety to men by increase of his intelligence. She awards sereneness, so she has been recognised as well wisher of all and that is why fair complexioned. Her costume is also white, the throne is of white lotus flowers and her conveyance is white duck.

Like other Gods, she has four hands. By two hands, she holds Veena (a string instrument) as the symbol of art, the third she has a book, which is symbolic of knowledge and in the fourth hand, she has a rosary of white Sapheetak (Lotus).

Post Vedic Saraswati is not only the Goddess of intelligence, knowledge and arts, but also the Goddess of sound (speech). this attribute of speech was acquired from R'GVEDIC VĀK.

R'GVEDA I.23.1.49 narrates,' Saraswati, that retiring breast, which is the source of delight, with which thou bestowest all good things, which is the container of wealth, the distributor of riches, the giver of food (fortune), that (bosom) do thou lay open at this season for our nourishment.'

IN YAJURVEDA, a yet another attribute of Saraswati is referred in a prayer to YAMARAJ:-

'I offer my prayer to you by the initiation of Savita, by medicines edited by Saraswati and produced by energy, for the prosperity in grains' (VINSHODHAYAE CHAP : 20).

VISHWĀMITRĀ'S CURSE

In a legend, described in VAMANĀ PURĀNA, (Chap 40), once enemity aroused between Vishwāmitrā and saint Vaśistā, because of interference in worship. Vaśistā had his Ashram at Sathanu, a place where Lord Sthanu had invoked Saraswati and where Dweswar had installed Linga and a huge Saraswati image. At that place, Vaśistā used to worship, which was not to the liking of Viśwāmitrā. So Viswāmitrā asked Saraswati to go and flow back Vaśistā in her waters, so that he could kill Vaśistā. Saraswati was in distress to undertake such as ordeal, but still Saraswati gave the message to Vaśistā. The latter agreed and requested Saraswati to flow him down to Viswāmitrā. This was done. Viśwāmitrā seeing Vaśistā, went in search of his dagger. Saraswati, out of fear and inorder to save a brahmin murder submerged Vaśistā in her waters. On seeing this, Viśwāmitrā was enraged and cursed Saraswati, 'O' flowing main river, because you have deprived me, therefore, henceforward, you will flow blood only in the region of the demons'. It became a boon for the demons, who drank blood and enjoyed on the banks of Saraswati. In due course, some saints reached the spot and were astonished to see the fate of such sacred waters. On hearing the tale of Saraswati, the saints prayed and visualised the formation of a sangam (Confluence of rivers: Gangas, Yamuna and Saraswati at Paryag: Allahabad).

Thereafter, all the demons took bath in the confluence and got rid of their evil doings and became purified.

In another version, when Saraswati flowed Vasistā to Viswāmitrā Vasista invited all the Gods and drew, into her stream, water from ARUNĀ (a river between the Saraswati and Drasdvati in Kurukshetra). When the Gods assembled, the installation of the image of the Goddess was set up and later the temple (Saraswati temple in Pehowa) was founded on 14th Chaitra (30-31 March). With the merger of Aruna river into Saraswati, the waters of the cursed Saraswati became immortal and the blood, which was food for the evil spirits, was purged away.

In the earlier mythology, the rakshasas (demons) seem to have been giants. It were they, who snatched the book of learning from Goddess Saraswati's hands, when she came down from the hills to the plains of Punjab (Thanesar). The loss of the book put her to great shame and she became a river, which sank into the earth, to come out at Sangam at Paryag (Allahabad).

SARASWATI AND RAMAYANA

Regarding the Story of epic RAMAYANA by Valmiki, a couplet describes, 'Once, when the poet Valmiki was bathing in the river Tamsa, he saw a pair of birds in a happy mood; but suddenly a hunter shot an arrow to the male bird and killed that. The female was heart broken at the loss of her mate and rent the sky with woeful cries.' Deeply moved by the lamenting cries of the female birds grief, valmiki quite unknowingly, cursed the hunter saying that the hunter would never have a peaceful life, as he had broken the home of innocent birds. After a little while, he realised that cursing did not behove a sage like him. Then B'rhma came to his rescue and explained that Goddess Saraswati had caused him to utter the verse to fulfill the curse of Bhrigu and further advised him to compose an epic on the tragic life and role of RĀMA in righteousness.

IN BUDDHISM

In Buddhism, Avalokitesvara is derived from the meditation of ADI BUDDHA, and cooperation in the creation of the world by giving his eyes to form the SUN and MOON, his teeth to form SARASWATI, Goddess of eloquence, and so on.

IN JAINISM

Because of the fact that Saraswati showed scant respect for B'rhma, she is respectfully honoured by the Jainās.

IN TANTRICISM

In Tantricism, Saraswati has also an important tantra. There are vaious scriptures on Tantra, which are known to the Sadhakas (devotees) one of them is Saraswati Tantra.

IN LITERATURE

Saraswati has always been referred to in literature, since Vedic age. Even in Assamese literature of modern period, she is included in the verse pertaining to Siva's marriage. In the song called 'HARA GAURIR BID', a reference to Laksmi and Saraswati shows these Goddesses coming to the marriage place with ornaments and presentations.

SAM VEDA

Sām Veda hymn 6(3) 13 (2) reads :-

'We, the wishers of mothers, wives and sons today, in obeisance to Saraswati, the one whose sisters are all the seven and Gāyatri and rivers like the Ganges, that Saraswati, who is truth for us all.'

ATHARVA VEDA

Rishi Atharvagira advises all those, who have dissident views to come to him and invoke heavens, where Saraswati, Indra and Agni are all present, for prosperity.' (6.10.64)

PRAYER

'O' Goddess Saraswati, your motherliness is peace giver, giver of comfort, the awardee of pious waters, nourishing and prayer worthy, May you give that boon to us '(R'GVEDA 7.1.10)

In another prayer vide R'GVEDA (7.1.11):-

'We pray to you (Saraswati) that your roaring thunders (moving over the whole universe, decorating the world and elctrified), may not destroy our fertility. They should cause no destruction amongest our progeny. The hot rays of the sun should not harm our crops. May you be so kind'.

SACRED SCRIPTURES:

MAHABHARATA: It is a salvation scripture or a sacred treatise, showing the way to salvation, expanding the highest religious philosophy of India and inculcating reverence, not only for NARAYANA, the supreme spirit, Saraswati from whom flow all knowledge, learning and the arts, and NARA, the superman, the ideal fighter and the seer, the close associate of God, but also for mankind in general. 'This is the holy mystery', declares the Santiparva of the great epic, 'There is nothing nobler than humanity' (XII. 299.20). It has been advised that MAHĀBHĀRATA, the scripture describing the victory over Asura's (demon's) realm, should be studied after paying homage to the supreme spirit Nārāyanā (Visnu) incarnation Sri K'rsna, his jewel of a man all time comrade Arjun, and to the one who gave exposure to the exploits and deeds of both, Bhagwati Saraswati and to the author Lord Vyāsā.

NARAYANI STUTI:

The Devi Saraswati, as depicted in this work has three major manifestations: Mahākāli, Mahā Laksmi and Mahā Saraswati. These aspects should not be confused with the Puranic deities Pārvati, Laksmi and Saraswati. They are actually the three major manifestations of the one superior power MAHESWARI, according to the three gunas (Tamas, Rajas and Sattva).

SARASWATI TANTRA

There are various scriptures on Tantra, among them one is SARASWATI TANTRA. 'TARA' was a purely Buddhist Goddess. Perhaps the hindu Tara is an entirely different Goddess. The name is a common epithet of all the great Hindu Goddesses as is seen in the SAHASRNAMA (Invocation of the thousand names) of

SARASWATI: THE GODDESS

LOLITA (Siva's spouse), of Saraswati and of Lakśmi, who have no relation to the Vajarayana, the Buddhist Goddess.

Since the Vedic times, Saraswati has been an important Goddess as a Goddess of River Saraswati and as such it is worthwhile studying the river Saraswati and her presiding deity Goddess Saraswati.

SARASWATI (UTTAR-PRADESH)

CHAPTER IV
THE RIVER SARASWATI

As River Saraswati, her importance is no less. In regard to the birth of a group of Vedic Gods in terms of the PURANIC versions, seven Maruts were born in Sapta Sarasvata, the part of the sacred river Saraswati, where there are seven branches.

In VAMNĀ PURĀNĀ (3.7-8, 34. 18-23, 36. 33-34) and VARAHĀ PURĀNĀ (97.15.16) in indian mythology throughout, it is believed that the image of fire placed in water, expresses control of indestructible excess energy. So when lord Siva wished to wash away his sin of brahaminicide, the immersed himself in the Saraswati river, but in vain. For the control of lust (sexual desire), there is a general precedence of submersion in water. MAHĀBHARATA epic (XII. 207.13) states,' Let a man, in whom passion has arisen, enter the water'.

INDUS SARASWATI CIVILISATION

A 5,000 years old Indus Saraswati Script wooden sign board, recently unearthed from DHOLAVIRA (Gujerat) in 1996, indicates that it was the origin of modern Indian, Aramaic and Greek scripts. Archaeologists have, therefore renamed the generally known Indus valley civilisation as the Indus Saraswati Civilisation. Nearly two thirds of Indus civilisation sites were on the banks of Saraswati river and only fiver percent along the Indus. The majority of the remaining sites are in Gujerat and Utter Pradesh, South and East of the Saraswati. Indus Saraswati script has been described as the originator, of which Brahmi, modern Devnagri and Tamil are all derivatives. The use of the script in India seems to have become rare after 2,000 BC and it is believed that this happened after the Saraswati dried up around the epic and people were forced to migrate out of the once rich region to other parts (The HINDU daily 13.08.1996).

During the third millenium BC, when a dry climatic period began in the modern belt of Asia, bands of the Aryans migrated from the grasslands and Steppes of Central Asia, riding horses and wheeled vehicles and gradually found themselves in the plains of the seven rivers called 'SAPTA SINDHU'. The seven rivers comprise either the seven streams of the Saraswati, or the five steams of the Saraswati referred to in the ATHARVEDA, alongwith the Ganges and the Yamuna.

In the ancient times, the Saraswati was a mighty river system that flowed westward into the gulf of KUTCH. But this river was captured by the sands of Rajputana (Rajasthan) and the main part of it flowed eastward and became the Yamuna. The Indo Aryans, first settled in the valleys of Indus, the Satluj, the Saraswati and the Drisadvati, before moving to the upper reaches of the Ganges and the Yamuna. The SARAYU marks the eastern most frontier of R'GVEDIC and the SADANIRA of later Vedic culture. From the Saptasaraswati to the Sadanira, was a long arduous march of the Vedic Aryans. among their Gods and Goddesses were included Saraswati, who was at the beginning a river deity and was worshipped later as the Goddess of learning and wisdom. The Saraswati, the river of the Bharatās, is constantly mentioned in connection with BHARATI, the personified divine protective power of the Bharatās. The Goddess BHĀRATI and the God AGNI were the guardians of the Bharatās, in their eastward expansion. Again Vaisvānara, according to the Vedic myth, travels eastward from the river Saraswati. Rivers cross his path, but AGNI burns on across all the streams. The spread of the Aryans to the quarters of the earth was symbolically the extension of the suzerainty of Saraswati or Bharati, the Goddess of the Bharatās.

SARASWATI IN R'GVEDIC PERIOD

Originally, Saraswati of R'GVEDA period, was a vast river, which originated form the Himalayas flowed through modern Harayana and Rajasthan, to the sea. The dry part of this ancient river can still be seen to the west of THANESAR (Punjab) and spreading near Sohava, (SIRSA), passes to Hanumangarh in Rajasthan and still further to its end in the desert land of Suratgarh.

During R'GVEDA period, this river was as revered as the modern Ganges today. Vedic hymns were composed, many yageyas were performed on its banks. Literature and arts took their birth. Gradually Saraswati became the goddess of knowledge and the arts.

R'GVEDA (Bhiteye Mandal 41 hymn), In this hymn Saraswati is invoked by Rishi Gulsamad thus:-

'O' Supreme among mothers, supreme in rivers, supreme among Goddesses, we are without admiration, May you make us praise worthy.

As knowledge makes a man admirable, so Saraswati has been identified as the giver of knowledge. R'GVEDA (7.35) 1May Saraswati bless us with the award of knowledge.

Saraswati river, also called B'RHMA NADI, PRAHLAD, the king of demons alongwith others form Netherworld, went ton a pilgrimage to Nemisharneye and there they saw the sacred waters of river Saraswati. Prahalad asked Chavan rishi, as to what are the pilgrimage places on earth, in space and in the Nether world. Chavan replied that on earth there is one Namesharneye pilgrimage and the other PUSHKAR in space, CHAKRA pilgrimage in the Netherworld. Prahalad with his comrades visited Namesharneye and saw the sacred, pure waters of Saraswati (a river of B'rhma) in the heavens. on the banks of the river, he met NARĀ and NARĀYANĀ, whom he gave a grim fight but lost in the end. (VAMANĀ PURĀNĀ). Mahrishi LomHarshana describing the origin, pilgrimage place, its appearance and disappearance of Saraswati river said, 'This old stream originated From Palaksha tree. It has been recognised as a special one among the rivers. Even if a person repeats its name regularly daily, even then this river gives the relief from their sins. Such is her compassion. this river, cutting through thousands of hilly tracts, enters the forest of the demons. Its water is considered utmost holy and virtuous. Mahamunindra Markandeye, seeing that river in the tree Palakheye, had taken it out from a vein and then praised the stream, 'O' Goddess, you are the mother of all lokās (Times) and extremely welfare benevolent. O' Goddess, your status is one, which can bestow salvation, to the true and the untrue. Your waters are of the same kind as of the sea. They are imperishable, ultimate B'rhma.'

Just as fire is latent in the wood, but it appears to no one, similarly B'rhma is latent in you, as also the whole universe. O'Devi, where there is stable and unstable word 'AUM', there only are three scales, which are and are not. There are three Lokas (worlds). VEDAS are also three (fourth is a later one), there are three kinds of knowledge and three types of fire. There are three lights and DHARMA (religion), wealth and fortune, functions are also three. Sattva, Rajas and Tamas are also three. There are three classifications (castes) and B'rhmā, Visnu and Mahes (Siva) Gods are also three. There are three metals and three states of matter. There are three manes and three molecules. 'O Mother Goddess, this jumble of three is also yours. You have different kinds of appearences. You are spiritual and eternal form of B'rhma. You are the SOMA institution, you are the oblation organisation and an institution for eternal sacridity. 'O Goddess, all these attributes, are recited by B'rhm devotees.

INVOCATIONS

In the valley of Gods, North Kaushal, this Saraswati was invoked by UDDHAK rishi and thus had come to that region, where tree bark and deer skin wearers, worshipped her and in Kedar, it was named holy MANOHARA.

Prajapati Daksheye, after Yajna, had created Saraswati Gangadhar Bhagwati Bimloda. Mahatma MANDKAN joined the various streams. It was brought to Kurukshetra, by Markandeye through worship of Kuru. As narrated in MAHĀBHĀRATA (Aadi Parva), Gandharva Raj Chitrangad, noticing that Shantanu's son chitrangad had been inflicting untold atrocities on gods, men and demons, fought with him for three years in Kurukshetra plains, on the banks of river Saraswati. Shantanu's son Chitrangad died at the hands of the Gandharv Chitrangad. DEV BRAT (Bhism patameh) went and completed the last rites of his brother and later installed Vichitra Veereye on the throne.

The river Saraswati, powerful and well established in towns, flows through them, as a pious river with sanctified waters. She is a charioteer for all rivers, which merge into it. That Saraswati, supreme of the rivers, which flows from the mountains to the sea, heard the propitiation of king NAHUSH and gave him prosperity and wealth. VAYU, the giver of rain, participated in the sacrifice. The performers of the sacrifice were awarded brave sons and purified their bodies. 'May the beautiful Saraswati, before whom the revered Gods bow, who is merciful to her devotees, listen to our invocation'. 'O Saraswati, we, who make sacrifice and pay homage, we reverentially may get wealth from you. May you accept our propitiation, then we will gain out of our labour. O' Saraswati, you are the bestower of great wealth. This devotee prays to you to give productivity to the performer and be our nourisher at all times (R'gveda 5.6.95)' 'O' purifying Saraswati, you are a bestower of wealth through wisdom, May you make this sacrifice, a success. The encourager of truth, the cultivator of great wisdom, May this Saraswati accept our sacrifice (yageye). Saraswati is the giver of vast sea of knowledge. She encourages all wisdom towards knowledge' (R'gveda 1.1.3.11)

'O' Saraswati, the supreme among mothers and the rivers, May she make us (poor) wealthy. O'Saraswati, you are lustrous; the productivity resides in you, May you be satisfied with Somā (divine juice). O'Saraswati, May you bless us like your sons. the supreme synthesis of food and water, May you accept our sacrifice. This sacrifice is enjoyable, the Gods wish it. The performers are Gritsad dynasty persons' (R'gVeda 2.4.41; 15-19).

SAMVEDA (6(3) 13(2)):-

'The creator, consort and those ambitious for sons, charitable ones reach and invoke Saraswati. The utmost dear GĀYATRI seven meters and the Ganga like all streams, who are all sisters to Saraswati, that Saraswati is TRUTH for us all. Those inspirers of intelligence SAVITA God, who is worshipful because of his truthfulness and lustre, we pray to him'.

R'G VEDA (6.5.52) :-

'May Saraswati river flow towards us for safety. She may give us relief by her medicines'.

TRIBUTARIES:

APAGĀ: One of the seven holy rivers in Kurukshetra. It is obviously the Āpayā of the R'GVEDA (III.23.4). According to Vamanā Puranā (36.1.4) it is the Krosa to the east of the village Mānusa. It has disappeared long ago. In its dry bed, a tank had been dug up and his been given the name of Āpagayā.

ĀPAYĀ : A river probably the tributary of the Saraswati. It flowed between Saraswati and the Drsadvati (R'gveda III. 34.4). According to Zimmer, it was a smaller tributary, which flows past Thanesar or the modern Indravati further west. Pischel assigns it to Kurukshetra, of which the ĀPAYĀ is mentioned as a famous river in the MAHĀBHĀRATA (III.83.68).

ARUNĀ : A river between the Saraswati and Drsadvati, near Prathudaka in Kurukshetra (Mbh IX. 43. 30-35). The Saraswati is said to have joined itself to Arunā, to purge the rakshasas of their sins and Indra of Brahmin murder (Mbh III. Chap 83.15). Its junction with the Saraswati, 3 miles to the North of Pehowā (Prthudaka) is called the ARUNĀ SARASWATI SANGAM (Padma Purana 1,27.39; Vamanā Puranā 40.43).

AMLU: A sacred river in Kurukshetra, probably a tributary of Saraswati (Vamanā Purana 37.7).

DRSADVATI: The first reference to this river is found in the R'GVEDA (III, 234) where it is mentioned alongwith Apayā and Saraswati, as a holy river for worship of AGNI. In the PAÑCAVIMŚA Brāhamana (XXV. 10.13) and later Drsadvati and Saraswati are the scene of special sacrifices. In MANU (ii. 17) these two rivers form the western boundary of the middle country. It is identified by some as Gaggin (Ghagar),which flows through Ambala and Sirhind (Harayāna) now lost in the sands of Rajputana (Rajasthan). It has also been identified with Raksi by Cunningham, which flows by the southeast of Thanesar. It formed the southern boundary of Kurukshetra (MbhIII. Chap 5.2). Lately it has been identified with modern Chitrang (Chautang or Chitang), which runs parallel to the Saraswati. The river flows through Phalaki Vana (Vamanā Puranā ch 36). According to Vamana Purana (Ch 34) KAUŚIKI was the branch of Drsadvati, mentioned in YOGIN TANTRA (2.5.139). MANUSMRITI declares that the country lying between the Saraswati and Drsadvati is called Brahmavarta and is built by Gods themselves. Brahmavarta was afterwards called Kurukshetra.

CHAPTER V
KURUKSHETRA

BRAHAMĀVARTA was the original name of KURUKSHETRA. The country between the rivers Saraswati and Drsadvati in the Eastern Punjab, where the Aryans first settled themselves. From this place, they occupied the country as Brahmarsidesa. It has been originally identified with Sirhind. Its capital was KARAVIRAPURA on the river Drsadvati according to the KALIKĀ PURANĀ (Ch 48-49) and Barhismati according to BHAGVATĀ PURANĀ (III. 22). The MEGHDUTA shows that Kurukshetra was a part of Brahmāvarta.

Listening to the appellations of Rishi Markandeye, that tongue of Visnu, Saraswati Goddess spoke, 'O' rishi, wherever you take me, I shall go there immediately. 'Rishi Markandeye appealed,' The most ancient primordial pilgrimage holy place is Brahmsār. It has been described as the heart of the snakes. Rishi Kuru has undergone severities and austerities, there, so that place is named Kurukshetra. You may pass through that range, and make it holy with your stream of sacred pure waters'.

Rishi Lom Harsha said that hearing the prayers of Markandeye, that stream appeared then in Kurukshetra. Gaining a ground there, Saraswati river then flowed towards the south. There are hundreds of pilgrimage places, which are served by the saints. A dip in the holy

SARASWATI

SARASWATI (BENGAL)

waters there, gets one riddance from allx sins. The very recitation of the names of these pilgrimages awards one sacridity.

SALVATION is of four kinds:-

1. To obtain knowledge about B'rhma
2. To worship the ancestors at Gaya pilgrimage.
3. To die in Grogrehe.
4. To live in Kurukshetra.

The internal portion of Saraswati and Drisadvati rivers, glorified by the Gods, is called Brahmvrat. To live on the banks of the river in Kurukshetra or to have the ambition of living in Kurukshetra, gains Braham knowledge. There is no doubt about it. The Gods, saints and the accomplished take holy water from there, which has the effect of an audience with B'rhma. One attains highest status by its waters. Such people are not afraid of worldly calamities or dark times. Those who die in Kurukshetra, they never degenerate. After a dip in Saraswati, if one worships Daksheye and makes offerings of flowers incense and conscientiously prays, ' I shall see these streams and tour these pilgrim places after your worship and blessings, May you remove my future obstacles'.

VAMANĀ PURĀNA describes,' Those people, who live on the south of Saraswati and on the north of Drsadvati i.e. Kurukshetra region, live in Swarga (HEAVEN). Even DHRITRASHTRA in Mahabharata, who was on the side of Daryodhan (sinful-untrue); described Kurukshetra as Dharamakshetra (Region of righteousness).

SUCH IS THE EXALTATION AND GLORY OF KURUKSHETRA.

KURUKSHETRA REGION

In the ancient past, in the midst of Kurukshetra, there were seven forests; the names of which are sacred and remover of sins. One is KAMYEK, the other ADITI forest, another VYASA and another of fruits. One is named SHEET Van (Cool forest), another forest is SURYA and the seventh is called MADHUVAN. These are now extinct because of urbanisation.

In addition to the seven forests, there were seven rivers; One is SARASWATI, the most merciful, the other VAITRINI, APAGA is very pious, Mandakini Ganga, MADHUSHRAVA AND AMLU are other rivers, KAUSHIKI river is the destroyer of sins. DRSDAVATI and HIRANEYETI rivers are also sacred. MAHABHARATA (VI.9.30;30) mentions some others rivers BRAHADADHVANI, BRHADVATI and CANDRAMA (Mbh VI.9.29). Except Saraswati, all other rivers only flow in the rainy season.

PILGRIMAGE

Among all pilgrimages, Kurukshetra pilgrimage is the most sacred like MANSAROVER amongst all lakes. Mansarover at an elevation of 15,000 feet, is a lake, which is the highest sweet water like in the world. Kurukshetra pilgrimage is like NANDAN forest among all flowering forests, TRUTH among all religious fundamentals, ASVAMEDHA among all sacrifices (Yageyas) and like VEDAS among all sacred scriptures and as MANUSMRITI among all Smiritis. (VAMANĀ PURĀNA). THANESAR (STHĀNESWAR), a place where temple of Mahādeva (Siva) exists, is more famous because of its link with Pandavas. All places near Sthāneswar, in the midst of Saraswati and Drsdavti rivers, are called Kurukshetra or the region of that Kuru king, of whom it is said, that he became an ascetic on the sacred lake in the south of the town. There are 180 pilgrimage places in this region; of which 91 are on the northern bank of Saraswati river. Counting the Vaisnuism places Naghrid on Punid; Vyassathal on Basthali; Prasar on Balu and places near Naran; pilgrim places in Kurukshetra are about 360.

There is a SHUKL Tirath (Pilgrimage), on the north of Sthānubutt. In the east of Sthānu batt, there is VYOM TIRATH. To the south of Sthānubatt, is DAKSHEYE TIRATH. In the west is Nakul's abode. Among all these holy places, in the centre is STHĀNU. By its very sight, one gains highest status and purity. On the 8th or 14th day, any person, who circumambulates this pilgrimage, gains SIDDHI (spiritual power). On the north of Sthānubatt, there is Mahālinga, installed by TAKSHAK, which is the fulfiller of all ambitions. On the east of the Batt, there is a great Linga, installed by VISWAKARMĀ. Seeing the face of the Lingā, one gins SIDDHI (Supernatural powers). There only is SARASWATI installed as YING LINGĀ. By worship of this Goddess, one gains wisdom and intelligence. In the region of the Batt, there is a Lingā, which was installed by B'rhma.

As we see today, the huge tank in Kurukshetra from east to west is 3546 feet long and 1900 feet wide. According to BRAH MIHIR of Abu Rihan, on the lunar eslipse, water from all rivers, flowed to Thanesar, so that pilgrims could have a dip in the holy waters, all at one time. This tank existed much before the Kauravas and Pandavas, becasue ancestors of both, KURU had entered into trance (Samadhi) on its banks. Parsuram (Visnu's incarnation) had massacred Kshatriyas here. It was here, where PURURAVA got his celestial consort laden with flowers in the company of four celestial deities. This tank is since R'GVEDIC period, because it was here that INDRA's horse faced thunderbolt, was ultimately traced. This is also possible that this tank is the same place where God Visnu had picked up his Discus to murder Bhismā. Indra had killed Vritas here and their bones (later called Pandavas) are seen here in Asthipur near Cakra Tirath (Thanesar tank). ABHIMANYU KHERĀ is a locality, also known as CAKRAVYUHA, five miles south east of Thanesar, where Abhimanyu, son of Arjun, was slain. Temples of ADITI and SURYA and a tank known as the SURYAKUNDA are of interest to pilgrims.

THANESAR is important for 'If a man be drowned and his body cannot be found, his relatives go to Thanesar and there make an effigy of him, which is duly cremated on the bank of the Saraswati at Thanesar, the last rites of the dead are recognised as having been completed.

BRAHMASĀRAS is a sacred lake in Kurukshetra near Thanesvara (Thanesar), mentioned in the VAYU PURANA (77.51); MATSEYE PURANA (22.12) and the VAMANA PURANA (22.55.60 and 49.38- 39). Its other names are RAMĀHRIDEYE and PAVANĀSARAS etc.

BRAHMODUMBARA is a pilgrimage place in Kurukshetra mentioned in the Mahabharat (III Ch 83.71).

CAKRA is an ancient Janapda near the Saraswati mentioned in Mahabharata VI. Ch 9.45 and Bhagawata Purana X. 78.19.

CAKRA TIRATHA on the Saraswati (Vamana Purana 42.5 57. 89; 81.3). It is Rāmāhrideye in Kurukshetra

DVIPĀYANAHRIDEYE is identified with RĀMĀ HRIDEYE. The lake was called Dvaipāyana Hrideye on account of an island in its centre. The isle is surrounded with Bankhanadi koel and Brahamani rivers. This island contains a sacred well CANDRAKUPA, which was visited by pilgrims form all parts of India, at the time of the eclipse of the moon.

CATURMUKHA is a pilgrimage place on the Saraswati, as mentioned in Vamana Purana Ch 42.28.

ASVINOSTIRTHA is a place in Kurukshetra region, mentioned in the Mahabarata III Ch 83.17.

AUŚANASA is sacred tirath on the bank of the Saraswati (Mahabarata III 83.135 and Mataseye Purana 22-31); also called KAPALA MOCANA tirath (Mahabharat 39.9.22). The Vamana Purana (39.1 & 14.42.24) states that the sage UŚANAS attained perfection (SIDDHI) here and became the planet VENUS.

AVAKIRAN is a pilgrim place under Kurukshetra and the Saraswati (Vamana Purana 39. 24-35). Bakadalbhya, who begged of DHRITRĀSHTRA and when condemned by the latter, made the whole of Dhritrashtra territory an Ahuti (ashes) in Prthudaka. The Mahabharata (IX Ch 41.1) and the PADMA PURANA (1.27.41-45) state that it is Darthin, who is mentioned as one, who brought the four seas.

BADARIPĀCANA is sacred tirath under Kurukshetra. Sage Vaśiśtha had his ashram there, as mentioned in the Mahabharata (III. 83, 179-182; IX 47.33 and 48.1 and 51).

BENEFITS FROM THE BATH

Benefits from a dip in the sacred rivers in Kurukshetra and a pilgrimage to these holy places are immense. First of all, one should pay obeisance to the door guardian

SARASWATI

SARASWATI — KALAMKARI STYLE (SOUTH)

RANTUK and then worship DAKSHEYE and then start on the pilgrimage to other places. First of all visit Aditi forest, where the mother of Gods ADITI had undergone austerities for getting a son. After a bath there and offering prayers to Aditi Goddess for getting a son, (a son who shall be as much enlightened as a hundred adityas: Gods), go to Visnu place, a reputed place where God is vested. Then visit other places, make offerings and prayers. the benefit of a dip in holy waters and a pilgrimage to various places in Kurukshetra awards one happiness, prosperity and children; as also is worshipful for the ancestors. Saraswati's blessings for intelligence wisdom and knowledge are obtained.

LORD KIRISHNA MUSEUM

A museum, exclusive devoted to the multi-dimensional life of Lord K'RSNA has been set up in Kurukshetra, which is a singular distinction of its kind in the world. The artefacts displayed in the museum represent K'rsna as a revered God, an incarnation of God VISNU, a great philosopher, an astute statesman of the battle of Mahābhārata and above all a supreme lover. Multifaceted personality of K'rsna, episodes of his childhood, pranks and exploits, miracles, Rasa lila, philosophy and message on the three cardinal yogas (Bhakti devotion); Jnana (Supreme knowledge) and KARMA (desireless action) have been exhibited. Rare manuscripts, paintings, wood carvings, Sculptures, etchings on palm leaves, papier mache and findings belonging to the age of K'rsna including excavated material from Dwarda, Mathura and Kurukshetra, are a rare sight for the visitors and the pilgrims.

GĀYATRI
(stone Padmanābhasvāmi temple, Trivandrum)

CHAPTER VI
TRIPLE DIVINITIES AND SUN GOD

R'g Veda 3.62 gives a hymn called SĀVITRI. It is celebrated meter of Vedas of twenty-four letters in three lines, addressed to the SUN GOD SAVITR. SĀTAPATHA Brāhamana (C.13.19) identifies this hymn as well as the meter with AGNI.

The GĀYATRI meter was regarded so holy that it was described as 'The MOTHER OF THE VEDIC METERS'. In due course Gāyatri was regarded as the mother of the Vedas (Veda Mātā). AITRYA BRĀHAMANA (5.27) while narrating the story of bringing Some (symbolic of Sun's brilliance) down to the earth, symbolises speech (VĀK) as a pretty lady, identified with the hymn; Vāq Vai GĀYATRI (Chhandayoga Upanishad).

Thus GĀYATRI, SĀVITRI and SARASWATI, were visualized as triple divinities associated with the SUN God, as the three forms of the Sun during the course of a day and worshipped in the morning, midday and evening respectively.

The three lines (Padas) of Gāyatri hymn are identified with the morning Sun (Gāyatri); the Feminine counterpart of B'rhma; the midday Sun (Sāvitri, the feminine counterpart of Visnu) and the evening Sun (Saraswati as the counterpart female of Rudra Siva).

SARASWATI

GĀYATRI
(stone, Meenakshi temple, Madurai)

GĀYATRI

Gāyatri, a particular method of meditation, is symbolically represented as a Goddess with five heads and ten hands and holding nine weapons in all the hands except one. It should be borne in mind that Hindu imageries are purely symbolic, and a correct understanding of the symbolism is absolutely necessary for understanding and appreciating the subtle ideas expressed by the great Saints. In Hindu mythology, the human body is comprehended as representing the UNIVERSE a miniature cosmos. Ancient Hindus, therefore declared cryptically that an entire universe exists in an atom and went on repeating that a man should not waste his precious life, but should 'look inside' and realise what he is. The fact that God creates human machine is remarkable in one way. It hardly stops functioning right from the stage of conception to the stage of death. Thousands of miles of nerves link the heart, lungs, brain and other organs of the body. The nerves working properly activate the muscles. The chanting of Gāyatri mantra preceded by necessary anganayasa (touching of the parts of the body) is very much subtle in its effect on the human body, particularly in the context of spiritual elevation. ANGANAYASA, the act of touching the various nerve centres, achieves the purpose of activating these centres, which become ready for receiving sound vibrations generated by Gāyatri Mantra.

GĀYATRI MANTRA (HYMN)

Every religion has one chief mantra, as 'KALMA in Islam'; 'BAPTISM in Christianity; 'NAMO - ONKAR in Jainism'; 'HOON' of 'AUM' in Tibetans. In Indian religion (Dharma); the chief mantra is Gāyatri mantra. Casteism has no effect on it (all can recite it). It is to be chanted openly and not whispered in ears; its composition is neither male nor female; it is not restricted to any one country or region. Gāyatri hymn, in the primordial days of creation, manifested on B'rhma, who sermoned it by his four mouths in the form of four VEDAS. Rishi (Saint) Viśwāmitra is the composer author of the hymn.

In iconogrāphy, Gāyatri, has one face, two hands, in which she holds a water jub (kamandal) and a book symbolic of knowledge and science. Five faced and ten handed images are only symbolic of Śakti.

GĀYATRI GODDESS is a benevolent mother full of pardon and compassion. She is happy to listen to the lisping sound of her child. She is such a KĀM DHENU cow, who does not know how to injure others.

GĀYATRI and GANGĀ, both relieve the devotee of all sins and award liberation. The power (Śakti) of God Viṣnu is contained in them. They are both equal in fulfilling the desires of the devotees. Any human being, who is devoid of the worship and obeisance to these two, is a deprived person. Gāyatri is the creator of all meters and the Ganges is the mother of all lokas (ages). These two are the cause for the destruction of all evils (sins).

That Gāyatri protected the Gayas (which produce sound) and all the organs, the vital power within the body, Gāyatri came to be so called (protector of the organs: Gayas), because it protected the organs of the priests, who recite them. Gāyatri is the vital power which protects the organs (body) of the pupil from falling into hell and other dire calamites.

TRIPLE DIVINITIES AND SUN GOD

An eulogistic story on the knowledge of the Gāyatri as given in BRIHAD ARANYAK UPANISHAD (Ch 5.15) is that King JANAK asked Ashwatarashvi's son Bdila, why he, the knower of Gāyatri, was acting to the contrary by carrying him as an elephant (gift). Bodila replied that was due to his ignorance of the mouth of Gāyatri. The king then said, 'FIRE (AGNI) is the mouth of Gāyatri. One, who knows that fire is the mouth of Gayatri, burns like fire all the sins committed by him due to acceptance of gifts etc; that knowledge makes him clean, pure and free from decay as well as death.

The Gāyatri hymn is eulogized as comprehending all the Vedic Gods. AGNI is the entrance (mouth), RUDRA is the topknot (Sikha); VISNU is the heart and B'RHMA the armour. The three lines of the hymn are identified with the counterpart of B'rhma, Visnu and Rudra, as Gāyatri, Savitri and Saraswati. Gāyatri verse is the most sacred verse of the VEDAS. It appears in R'GVEDA (iii. LXII. 10) and reads as follows

'TAT SAVITUR VARENYAM,

BHARGO DEVASYA DHIMAHI,

DHIYO YO NAH PRACHODAYAT'.

Which menas, We meditate on the adorable light of the effulgent deity. May He, illuminate our intellect'.

Gāyatri is the chief of the meters and has three feet, each of eight syllables. The first foot 'TAT SAVITUR VARENYAM' has eight syllables just as Bhumi (Earth), Antariksha (Sky) and Dyaus (Heaven). Hence the earth, sky and heaven constitute the first foot of Gāyatri. He, who knows first foot of Gāyatri (consisting of these three worlds) conquers as much as there is to be conquered on earth, sky and the heaven.

The second foot 'BHARGO DEVASYA DHIMAHI' has eight syllables just as in R'GVEDA (Richah), YAJAR VEDA (Yajumshi) and SAMA VEDA (Samani). These three Vedas constitute the second foot of the Gāyatri hymn. He, who knows the second foot of Gayatri, consisting of three Vedas, obtains as much knowledge as can be obtained from the three Vedas. The THIRD foot 'DHIYO YO NAH PRACHODAYAT' has also eight syllables, as in 'prāna', 'Apāna' and 'Vyāna', the three forms of vital power. He, who knows the third foot of Gāyatri, conquers all creatures that exist in the universe.

The three footed Gāyatri, consisting of the gross and subtle universe rests on the celestial foot, the fourth (Turiya) the 'SUN', which is apparently seen. That fourth foot, the SUN (high above the sky), that shines on the entire universe, is created out of Rajas. He, who realises the fourth foot of Gāyatri shines like the sun with splendour and forms. Strength is the support of truth. The vital power is strength. Hence truth rests on the vital power. Thus the Gāyatri rests on the vital power that is within the body. Therefore Gāyatri is the protector (saviour) of the organ.*

Gāyatri Sāvitri and Saraswati, these three Goddesses represent the presiding deities of the famous Gāyatri mantra, chanted three times a days:-

GĀYATRI, presiding deity of morning prayer, rules over the R'GVEDA and gārhapatya.

---

* For a greater study of GAYATRI MANTRA, a reference to th author's book 'HINDUISM' 'Appendix' can be made.

TRIPLE DIVINITIES AND SUN GOD

SĀVITRI, presides over noon prayer and rules over the YAJUR Veda and the Daksinā fire.

SARASWATI, is the deity presiding over the evening prayer, rules over the SĀMAVEDA and the Āhavantya fire. She has one face and four arms and rides over Garuda.

Gāyatri mantra should be recited keeping meditation on B'rhma in the umblicus region, on visnu in the heart and on Siva in the forehead and also having thoughts on sun like par B'rhma. Gāyatri, the morning sun, representing R'GVEDA and B'RHMA, is a red complexioned young girl (kumari) who is two armed, carrying rosary (Aksa sutra) and ritual water pot (Kamandal) and riding upon a swan (Hamsa). DHAYANA SLOKA in DEVI BHAGWATA (12.3) gives a familiar iconographic representation of Gāyatri as a Goddess. It prescribes five faces, each with a different colour viz colour of pearl (mukta), coral (Vidruma), golden (hema) blue and white. Each face has three eyes. She carries in her hands two lotuses, discus, conch, trident, skull cup and a boon bestowal. She is bedecked with all ornaments and her be jewelled crown is decorated with crescent moon.

Yet another DHAYĀNA SLOKA mentions her body colour as bright red and she wears garlands of fresh red flowers. She is seated on a lotus. A third DHAYĀNA SLOKA describes her as fair complexioned and wearing red coloured silken garments.

A prayer to Gāyatri in ATHARVA VEDA (19.6.71) reads, 'O' Mother of the Vedas, invoked by me, May ye bless me with long age, breath, society, animals, honour, wealth and B'rhm knowledge and then depart to B'rhmlok'.

GĀYATRI AND B'RHMA

PADMA PURANA relates a story to explain how Gāyatri became associated with B'rhma. During a sacrifice (Yageye), when the appointed time for initian drew near, the priest beckoned to B'rhma (who was the chief performer) and his consort Saraswati to make haste. B'rhma arrived atonce but Saraswati tarried. In order to perform the ritual of initian at the auspicious hour. B'rhma had to sit with another woman brought by Indra. This woman could not be anyone else but his consort. So B'rhma formally married that woman (Gāyatri) by Gandharva rites. that woman was a cowherd maid, selling milk on the streets. After marrying B'rhma, she became Gāyatri, the purifier of the whole world. Later when Saraswati arrived, she was enraged and cursed B'rhma to be worshipped, no more than once a year.

SAVITRI

Another Sun Goddess is Savitri, who is invoked to shower her splendour in the famous Gāyatri hymn. Savitri is verily Gāyatri, because Gāyatri is the vital power.

R'GVEDA (II.4.6):-

'In truth, the divine Savitri, the the bearer (of the world) has perpetually been present for the generation (of mankind) for such is her office: verily she grants wealth to the pious (worshippers): May She, therefore bestow upon the performer of the oblation (sufficent) for his well-being.

The divine, vast handed 'SAVITRI', having risen, stretches forth her arms for the delight of all; the purifying waters(flow) for (the fulfilment of) his rites, and this circumambient air sport (in the firmament).

'The moving (sun) is liberated by his rapid rays; verily he has stopped the traveller from his journey: He restrains the desires of warriors for combat, for night follows (the cessation of) the function of Savitri.

'The engendered domestic radiance of AGNI spreads through various dwellings, and presides over all (sort of sacrificial) food; the mother (DAWN), has assigned to her son (AGNI), the best portion (at sacrifices) which is the manifestation of him, imparted by Savitri.

'The warrior, eager for victory, who has gone forth (to battle), turns back; (for) home in the desire of all moving beings: abandoning his half wrought toil, the labour returns home when the function of the divine Savitri (is suspended).'

'The animals search in dry places for the watery element, which has been collected in the firmament by thee: the woods are assigned (by thee) to the birds: no one obstructs these functions of the divine Savitri'.

'The ever going VARUNA grants a cool, accessible and agreeable place (of rest), to all moving (creatures), on the closing of the eyes (of Savitri); and every bird and every beast repairs to its lair, when Savitri has dispersed (all) beings in various directions'.

'I invite to this place, with reverential saluations, for my good, that Divine Savitri, whose functions are neither Indra, nor Varuna, nor Rudra, nor Mitra, nor Aryaman, nor the enemies (of the Gods) impede'.

In R'GVEDA (1.1.7) AGNI has been applauded, 'THOU ART THE DIVINE SAVITRI', as the possessor of precious things and protector of men. 'May that desirable wealth, which is granted to us, (by) Savitri, proceed from the sky, from the waters, from the earth; and May the happiness (which belongs) to the race of those, who eulogise thee, devolve upon me, repeating diligently thy praises.

PRAYER

'May he, who is adored by men, the protector of the wives (of the Gods) preserve us, when worshipping him, who is auspicious, the object of the meditation, and the all wise: may we be the beloved of the divine Savitri, that we may (thence by successful) in the accumulation of wealth and the acquisition of cattle.'

'May, the divine Savitri, the benefactor of all men, come benignantly to our solemnity, together with the divinitiees of the earth, and do you, who are (always) young, willingly present at our sacrifice (yageye), exhilarate us, as (you exhilarate) the whole world,'

VĀG DEVI SARASWATI

Vāk Devi (Vāg Devi) of R'GVEDA becomes Saraswati in post Vedic period. Saraswati of post Vedic period attained Aakās Bhava title in KUMARSAMBHAVAM of Kalidasa, from the attributes of R'G VEDIC Vāk Devi. R'G VEDA (10.125.5) describes her invokation and power (Sakti) by a saint and Vāk says,' The gods and men, whatever they speak, that all I speak. The one to whom I bless, I make him enlightened. I make them advanced in knowledge and wisdom'.

TRIPLE DIVINITIES AND SUN GOD

In post Vedic period, Saraswati synthesised the attributes of R'G Vedic Saraswati and Vāk in her, and became a very important Goddess VĀG DEVI: The great saint Yageyvalkey, by the grace of SUN God, propitiated Vāg Devi Saraswati. He praised her: 'O' Mother of the universe, be kind to me - a stupid mind. By the curse of my guru (teacher) I have lost my memory and knowledge, therefore I am in distress 'O' the primordial God of learning,
• May you grant me knowledge; give me memory and donate me learning; give me status and strength to compose in poetics; which is the technique of the disciple. May you bless me with capability to compose scriptures; get respectable true disciples; status in the assembly of honourable people and capacity to think right. Whatever has been lost, May you restore that, just as Gods reliven those who have been reduced to ashes. I pray and invoke Vāg Devi Saraswati, who is the light of B'rhma, is the
• primordial founder of all learning, that Goddess, without whom the living world, remains under roots and that Goddess, who is the founder Goddess of speech. That Saraswati Goddess, who is the originator Goddess of white snow, white sandalwood flower, Indu, white lotus; I pray to that Goddess; that BHARATI, whose foundation is colon Zero and in vowel marks; I pray to her again and again. The one, without whom no numericals can be dealt with and the one who is the form of TIME(kal); I pray to that Goddess. That Goddess, who is in the form of interpretation and the one, who is the of founder of elaboration and the one, who is the reformer of misconception; I pray to her. The one, who is the power of memory, power of learning and the power of intelligence and the one who is the power of influence, wisdom and imagination; I pray to her'.

SARASWATI

SARASWATI - BENGAL

TRIPLE DIVINITIES AND SUN GOD

SANAT KUMAR requested B'rhma seeking knowledge from him. The latter was dumbfounded to explain. then B'rhma went to Sri K'rsna and K'rsna advised B'rhma to propitiate Vāg Devi Saraswati. Then B'rhma by the order of Pramatma, invoked Vāg Devi and then by her grace, B'rhma laid down excellent principles of knowledge.

When Vasundhara asked a question from Lord Visnu, the latter could not answer. He, then by the consent of Kashyap muni, invoked VāgDevi. Then he experienced the principles for the destrcution of misconception.

When saint VYĀSA questioned Vālmiki regarding a hymn in Purana, being unable to answer, Vālmiki remembered you (Vāg Devi). then he tried and gained pure perfect knowledge for the destruction of negligence (carelessness). VYĀSA having learnt that Purāna hymn, propitiated Vāg Devi and then worshipped her at Pushkar (near Ajmer) for a hundred years. After obtaining a boon from you, he became a great composer of poetry. Then he prepared parts of Vedas and scripted Purānas.

When Mahendra asked Lord Siva about elements of knowledge, then for a while, that God remembered you and only then, he could give the right knowledge. Mahendra asked Brihispati about the knowledge of words, he then worshipped you (Vāgdevi) at Pushkar. After gaining a boon from you a blessings on knowledge of words, he imparted that to SURESWAR and explained its full meaning.

'Those, who taught the disciples and those who undertake studies themselves, undoubtedly they must have revered you in their thoughts and then only they could make progress in their work. O'Goddess, you have been praised and propitiated by the saints and the men. You have also been invoked by the Gods and the demons, by Gods B'rhma, Visnu and Siva. the one, whom five faced Siva and four faced B'rhma had worshipped, how can me- a one faced man, invoke you.

Then invisible light spoke to Yageyvalkey, 'Your now become a good composer of poetry', and then the light disappeared towards Baikunthlok. Anyone, who recites the hymn by Yageyvalkeye, will become a good poet, a conversationalist like Birhaspati. Anyone, who is a great fool and devoid of intelligence, should undertake the recitation of the Hymn (GĀYATRI MANTRA) for one year, then he would become a great litereaur and a poet.

Such is the glory and benevolence of the triple divinities GĀYATRI SAVITRI AND VĀGDEVI SARASWATI.

CHAPTER VII

DYNAMIC FORM OF SOUND

Ancient Indian musicologists conceived and deified Nada as goddess Saraswati, symbolising HER as the dynamic form of the eternal sound. They hold that music is surcharged with the divine energy. NADA, the subtle inner sound, incessantly heard in the cosmos, behind the gross physical level, revealing itself in various forms at different planes of existence, which is intrinsic to the very creative process. 'Music of the spheres' heard in the innermost recesses of th heart, when the mind is full, is familiar to all MYSTICS, the world over and every religious tradition had a distinct way of expression, and what is common to all is that the experience always comes as a revelation and can never be mistaken for the sound audiable to the human ear.

Sound (Vak is the body of B'rhma (ultimate Reality) and it is from sound that the entire creation has issued forth.

Sound, defined scientifically as vibration, a particular range of which is audible to the human ear, but there are various ranges which are beyond human hearing viz energy. It is apparent that the cause of the entire creation is energy, which is the postulate of science. In religion, this is metaphorically describeed as the breath of the eternal B'rhma. The sounds, which manifested themselves at the

SARASWATI (BENGAL)

time of creation are the vedic mantras, which were heard by the Rishis, the mystic seers, in their moments of intuition so the Vedas are referred to as SRUTI.

The primordial sound resound, unceasingly within every particles of creation. It is heard in the innermost recesses of the soul generally, as a result of spontaneous spiritual exercises or sometimes when the mind is in deep concentration and it is an we inspiring and blissful experience. This is in the form of a revelation and is variously referred to as NADA, voice of god, the divine sound and the Music of the spheres, which leaves a lasting sense of peace in the person, who hears it and the experience is more Vivid and real than any sensory experience.

The earliest music form of the Hindu tradition is the Music of the SAMA VEDA in which the mantras are sung with precision and intonation.

Music (the blessing of Saraswati) and singing hymns in ceremonial worship and other ritualistic procedures have been devised by man, to aid mental concentration sot that the mind can transcend the material plane to the subtler levels, till it becomes in tune with the infinite. Sound is the power that can lead man back to the infinite, if only he understands how to use it. Saraswati, as her S'akti Maha Saraswati has given the energy for sound (VĀK) and that is why all musicians pray and worship her.

Music, the boon of goddess Saraswati, "gives soul to the universe, wings to the mind, flight to imagination, charm to sadness, gaiety and life to every thing. It is the essence of order and leads to all that is good, just and beautiful" (Plato).

Brāhmī

CHAPTER VIII
MAHĀ SARASWATI

Saraswati is a PURĀNIC deity, the personification of all knowledgearts, science, crafts and skills. Knowledge is the antithesis of the darkness of ignorance. Hence she is depicted as pure white in complexion and in attire., since she is the representation of all sciences, crafts, arts and skills. She has to be extraordinarily beautiful and graceful, according to her attributes. Clad in a spotless white apparel and seated on a lotus seat, she holds in her four hands a Vinā (lute), Aksamālā (rosary) and a Pustak (book). In some variations, Saraswati is shown as holding several other arms and objects, which are not in conformity with her functions of peace, literature, her subtle forms. That form holding arms and violent objects, is that of MAHĀSARASWATI.

MAHĀSARASWATI, is the third deity representing the Sattvic aspect of DEVI DURGĀ. She is bright like the autmn moon and has eight hands, five faces and even three eyes and a blue neck. In her eight hands, she holds the pāsā (noose), Ankusā (goad), Padma (Lotus), Trisula (trident), Sankha (Conch), Cakra (Discus), even a bell, ploughshare, bow and arrows. It is she, who manifests out of the physical sheath of Pārvati and hence known as KAUSIKI DURGĀ. She is the very personification of physical perfection and beauty. She is the power of work, order and organisation. In this case, she is the Mahāsaraswati aspect of Drugā or Pārvati.

SARASWATI

SARASWATI (TIBETAN)
SARASWATI — (BENGAL)

CHAPTER IX

WORSHIP AND PRAYERS

BRAHAMVEYVERTEYE PURĀNA (15: 1-7) lays down Saraswati Pooja Viddhan (ritual) and Mantra (Hymn):-

NARAYAN (Visnu) said, 'DURGĀ, the mother of Ganesa, Radha, Laksmi, Saraswati and Savitri, are five kinds of nature in the universe. Their worship was popular and their influence was wonderful. Their actions were reformatory and the giver of all auspiciousness. These were the elements of nature and of arts and their character utterly pious. First of all, the worship of Saraswati was originated by Sri K'rsna, that Saraswati, by whose blessings, even the stupid become great pandits (literary).

Saraswati Goddess is far coloured, her form is attractive. She has a smiling face. Her body glitters much more than the rays of crores of moons. Saraswati Goddess is worship worthy of B'rhma, Visnu and Siva. Meditating on her in these reverential thoughts, I pray to that Goddess, who is invoked by saints, MANU and men. By chanting her original hymns, oblations should be offered. Then the devotee should prostate in front of her. For those, who adore her as their personal Goddess, it is a daily prayer.

RITUAL OR WORSHIP

The ritual of worship is :- In the month of Jan-Feb (Magh). on the fifth day of moonlit half of lunar month and on the day of the commencement of education, before noon, the devotee should become conscientiously purified. After bath and daily routine, he should, in all reverence instal the GHAT (symbolic). Then he should worship the six Gods viz: Ganesa, Surya(Sun), Agni, Visnu, Siva and Siva's consort Gauri (Pārvati). After that, he should then worship his personal God. Then, with reverence to his well known God, he should instil life into the GHAT and worship with sixteen rituals according to the VEDAS, with oblations.

SARASWATI HYMN AND ITS IMPORTANCE

The best appropriate basic hymn is Vedic eight worded Gāyatri Mantra. Otherwise to those, to whom any hymn has been prescribed by his Guru, for them that very hymn is the basic hymn (mantra). Saraswati word should prevail all over in the atmosphere. In the end 'SHRI HAVIN SARASWATI SWAHA' should be chanted. This mantra is the one, which fulfills all desires of the human mind. This hymn, which is the tresure of Narayan (Visnu), was first given to Valmiki on the banks of the holy Ganges in the pious region of India. BHRIGU gave this hymn to SHUKRA on Surya festival and MAREECH had gladly given this to VĀKPATI on the moon festival. B'rhma, utterly pleased initiated this mantra and instilled it in Bhrigu in Badrika Ashram. JAGATKARU gave a sermon on this hymn to ASTIK near Kshir sea. VIBHĀNDIK taught this mantra to Rishi (Saint) SRANG on the Meru mountain region. SIVA God gave a lesson on this hymn to Kanadmuni Gautam. SURYA (Sun) awarded this hymn to Yageyvalkey and Kātyyan.

LORD VISNU gave a sermon on this hymn to Pānini and Bhārdwaj; and in Bali's assembly in SATLOKA to SĀKDAYAN.

OBLATION

The oblation should include milk curd, Kheer (rice cooked in milk); fried rice, ladoos of til (sesamum), sugar cane juice, other sweet estables of white colour, jaggery, sugar, white rice powder, Bannana paste, white scented ghee, flour paste fried in ghee, Coconut sweets, fried bannana in coconut juice, sweet berries and other white fruits grown in the country. These should be reverentially offered according to one's capacity. White flavouring flowers and scented sandalwood, new white garments, conch, garland of white flowers, white ornaments, should be offered. Rituals prescribed in sacred scriptures should be religiously observed.

PRAYERS

Goddess Saraswati is the first to be worshipped in a yageye (sacrificial fire). R'GVEDA (10.17.7) lays down that obeisance to Saraswati is done first of all before beginning of a'yageye and that those who truly worship Saraswati are blessed by her boon.

ATHARVA VEDA (7-68.3) gives a prayer:-

'O' merciful Saraswati Bhagwati, thee bless us,

With comfort and well being,

And that we should never be debarred from your blessings'.

R'G VEDA (1.164.49) reads:

'O' Saraswati mother, gives us thy milk of abundance,

Comfort and riches,

Which fulfill all human desires.

A prayer in Atharva Veda (7.57.1) prays that one should seek the blessings of mother Saraswati and request for a boon to cure heart stricken tension and discomfiture.

R'G VEDA (7.5.57), 'That organ (body) of mine, which has become functionless, because of lack of food and the mind, which is under strees and strain, because of unsuccessful prayers, May Goddess Saraswati, show me the right path'.

Atharva Veda (7.1.10):- 'O' Goddess Saraswati, Thy boons are peace giving, merciful, pious, nourishing and praiseworthy. May, thee bless us with these'. Another prayer in Atharva Veda (7.1.11) is for the protection of crops: 'We pray to Goddess Saraswati that her wide spread thunders, fast blowing and lightening, which impart light to the whole world, may not destroy our crops. We. the devotees may not be harmed by these. The strong rays of sun, may not injure our crops. We pray to you for all this'.

R'G VEDA (III.1.4):-

'May BHĀRATI, associated with the Bharatas (Vach: speech); ILA (prithvi-earth) with the gods and men, and AGNI; and Saraswati (middle region) with the Saraswati as, may the three Goddesses sit down upon the sacred grass (strewn) before them'

This is interpreted as the Goddesss with heaven, mid heaven and earth or with speech or sound in the three regions.

R'GVEDA (II.1.3.8):-

'May the three Goddesses Saraswati (perfecting our understanding); the divine ILĀ and all impressive

WORSHIP AND PRAYERS

BHĀRATI; having come to our dwelling. protect this faultless rite, (offered) for our welfare.'

R'GVEDA (10-6.17):-

Those, who make sacrifice to Gods, invoke Saraswati and worship her. When the sacrifice commences, then the sacrifices invoke Saraswati. 'MAY Saraswati fulfill the desires of this donor. May, You come on a chariot alongwith the ancestors and participate in the Yegeye gladly. May You bring us freedom from disease and give us food. 'O' Saraswati, ancestors sitting on the south of Yageye, invoke thee. May You produce wealth and food for the donor. May You purify us in you nourishing waters (Ghee like) and wash our sine. May the God of waters wash away our bad deeds, so that we may not remain dirty (sinful) after purification by thou waters'.

WORSHIP SEASON

Out of six seasons in India, Sharad (Winter) and Basant (Spring) are the best, because in these two seasons, neither there is much cold not heat. Since ancient times, on the ninth of Ashwin (september) moonlit half of lunar month, Saraswati worship had been commenced and education started; but now on Nava Ratri (sep- Oct), on the ninth day Durgā worship is done, so at present Saraswati worship is undertaken on the fifth of Magh (February) moonlit half of lunar month.

SARASWATI (BENGAL).

CHAPTER X
FESTIVALS AND FAIRS

All Hindu festivals have a deep spiritual import or high religious significance. All such festivals have religious, social and hygienic elements in them. To mediate continuously is not possible for the majority of men. Hence special days in the year are set apart for worship, meditation and social meets, called festivals. India is unique in the celebration of festivals festivals, India is unique in the celebration of festivals (UTSAVA) and has a longer list of such days of rejoicing, as compared to anyother country of religion.

There are different seasons of rejoicing, qualified by fasts (upavāsa, Vrata), vigils (jagran), seasons of mortification and season of fructification of crops.

Most of the festivals are fixed to take place on certain lunar days, each lunation or period of rather more than twenty seven days, fifteen of which during the moon's increase, constitute the light half of the month, and the other fifteen the dark half. Some festivals are regulated by the supposed motions of the sun.

PEHOWA TEMPLE

In Saraswati temple at Pehowa, two fairs are held on Chet 1st (Feb-Mar); Chaturdashi Krishnapaks and Kartika

Shuklpaksha. CHATURDASHI in Chaitra (Feb-Mar) is also called PISHĀCHMOCHINI (riddance from evil spirits). As described earlier, on account of curse by Vashwāamitra, the waters of Saraswati river at Pehowā, had been turned into blood. Later by drawing waters of Aruna river into Saraswati river and on request by Saint Vashista to the Gods, the waters of Saraswati became pure and sacred. A festival is, therefore held in reverence to that and also that a Saraswati temple was set up at Pehowa on that date. An offering to ancestors (pindodakarna) on that date at the temple and the stream, according to Hindu belief, releases the souls of pitras (ancestors) from pretayoni (world of the dead) and gives them moksha (emancipation).

The second fair at Pehowa temple is held in the Krittikanakshatra puranmasi and to bathe in the Saraswati in that period, gives health, wealth, prosperity and birth of children.

FESTIVAL: VASANTA PAÑCAMI, on the fifth of the light half of Magh (Feb) is a spring festival, celebrated in the Punjab and northern states of India, when the fields are yellow with ripe mustard crop, the cold weather starts fading away and is the ideal time for the festival and kite flying thereon. Yellow garments are preferably put on and yellow rice is cooked, keeping in with the season. Saraswati pooja is done in educational institutions.

Vasanta Pancami is a spring festival, held in the month of Māgha (Feb-Mar) on the fifth of the light half of the month. In Bengal Saraswati (Sri), Goddess of arts and learning, is worshipped on this festival. No reading or writing takes place on this day ; and the day is observed as a holiday in all public and mercantile establishments, especially in educational institutions. The worship of Goddess Saraswati is performed, either before an image of the Goddess, or by placing books, reading and writing material, account books, pen and ink, in a purified place and the worship of the Goddess is done, as the items representing the image of the Goddess. Sometimes an official priest is called in, who reads the prescribed formulae, and presents rice, fruits, sweetmeats, flowers etc. to the Goddess and then distributes them among the devotees. The worshippers prostate before the image or stands before the image, with flowers in their hands, beseeching the Goddess to grant them the blessings of learning, intelligence, wealth, fame and health. The educational institutions, set up a large image of the Goddess, invite the patron and management committee members to attend and do honour to the Goddess. Money is usually gifted at this time, which becomes an annual income of the priest. A favourite offering is of sweet yellow berries. The students do not taste berries before this occasion.

SARASWATI - BENGAL

CHAPTER XI
LEARNING AND LITERATURE

Those whose are wise, they only make a ground for play and make houses. They, only can diagnose disease and can use suitable remedy. By intelligence, one gains wealth and wisdom only results in welfare. The wisdom, intelligence are the boons of Goddess Saraswati.

From alphabet the sky; from sky the air; from air the fire; from fire the water and from water-the earth from this earth came the benevolent world. These worldly bodies merge in water. from water to fire, from fire to air, from air to the sky and from sky to the great God Parmatama (MAHABHARATA: Shanti PARVA). The root of the whole is an alphabet, the boon of goddess Saraswati, The MAHABHARATA (shanti Parv) narrates a legend about VĀG Devi Saraswati. Yageyvalkeye said, "IN ancient times, I undertook severe austerities in worship of lord Surya (Sun). One day, when pleased, He said, "I give you a boon to give, whatever you demand." In reply I said "I have no knowledge about YAJUR VEDA, KINDLY teach me that. "Then God Sarya said," I give you YAJUR VEDA; you open your mouth and VĀG Devi Saraswati will enter your body." As ordained by Suryā, I opened my mouth and Goddess Saraswati entered in. Immediately on her entry, I felt a burning in my body and I jumped into water. Seeing me under pain, Surya said, "wait a little more and then you will fell peaceful". After a while, when I was calm, the God said, "you will soon be a litereur in all VEDĀS and UPANISHĀDS. Then your intelligence will rest in liberation, as is aimed at by yogis (saints).

After God Surya left, I came home and remembered Saraswati. On my rememberance, the Goddess appeared before me, adorned by vowels (Swar) and consonants (vyanjan) with Om ( ) in front then invoking HER and God Saryā, I meditated on them. At that time with great pleasure, I compiled SHATPAT with complete mystery and mythological assertions. Then my one hundred disciples learnt that SHATPAT from me. Thus from Suryā, I learnt the elements of penetration (birth and death).

Vasant Panc'mi festival, (briefly described chapter IX) falls on the 5th of Magh Shukl, in the most pleasant season 'Vasant' described as the king of seasons, which Lord K'rsna included in his magnificence as 'Ritunan Kusumākar'. This festival has been recognised as worshipful in reverence to goddess Saraswati since the Vedic and Puranic period. This is the day on which B'rhma, in order to break away the dry flatness in the world, created Saraswati and giving her a veena in hand, desired that SHE should award speech to the world. So Saraswati is called VEENA VADINI and VANI DAYANI (THE player on Veena and the giver of speech). By the pleasure of Saraswati, not only man but even gods gain discretion, wisdom, status, brilliance, music, speech, poetry and differentiation between proper and improper. That's why adoration to Saraswati is done at the time of Vasant Panc'mi festival. With the observance of 'Vasantey Brahmin moopneyt' ritual, children of the brahmins were initiated into learning and discipleship on this day. Sri K'rsna had also performed Saraswati's worship on this day, by virtue of

LEARNING AND LITERATURE

which he become perfect in sixteen arts and whole learning. In the ninth Skand of Sri DEVI BHAGWAT PURAANA, worship ritual of Saraswati is given, by reciting which anyone can become equal to BRIHASPATI (teacher of gods) and the greatest fool of all fools, can become highly literary. These mantras have been given under 'PRAYER' (CHAPTER IX). It is said that NARAYAN (VIS'NU) had sermoned these mantras to saint Valmik on the ganges, by virtue of which he became a great poet. Similarly Parsu Rām (incarnation of Vis'nu) blessed this mantra to Shukrac'arya (the priest of demons) in Pushkar region. B'rhmā imparted this hymn to Bhrigu muni, S'ankara (Sivā) to kanav saint, Jarārkāru saint to Asteek, and Surya god initiated yageyvalkey and Kātyyan into this. By the influence of Saraswati worship Vyāsa, in lighter moods, composed eighteen PURĀNAS.

The scientific reason for the celebration of this festival is that it gives us an indication to bring about a change in our food, clothing and outdoor activities. This is a festival of great importance to one and all especially to those concered with learning art, sciences and performing arts. This day is also to be remembered because on this day the brave child Hakikat Rai gave up his life to safeguard Hinduism and in the present times, the national poet NIRALA cleared the line of modern poetry and composed RAM KATHA' worship of international fame.

SARASWATI (NORTH)

CHAPTER XII
PILGRIMAGE, TEMPLES AND SHRINES

Afters pilgrimage to SOMA TIRATHA, there is SAPT SARASWAT, unique even in TRILOKI (three worlds). Saraswati river flows there as a confluence of seven rivers viz: Suprabhā, Kancanksi, Bimala, Manas, Halda, Sarasvatoya, Suvaran, and Vitalodka (Vamana Purana). Saraswati river is not visible there. Bhagwan Parmeshti, after prayers had invoked Saraswati. By B'rhma's wishes, this Suprabha Goddess Saraswati, became popular at PUSHKAR, on the earth.

By the sight of this fast flowing Saraswati river, the saints rejoiced. The saints revered that Goddess, who honoured B'rhma. Thus this Saraswati river established itself at Pushkar (near Ajmer). From there, it was brought to Kurukshetra by the prayers of saint Markandey, as described earlier. Rishi LOM HARSHA said, 'Where there is Saraswati, there the yageye (sacrifice) brings fruit'. Learning this, many saints and rishis assembled there and all of them invoked Goddess Saraswati. On the appellations of all assembled saints, Goddess Saraswati participated in the Yegeye. She was named KĀNCHANĀKSHI. Submerged Saraswati waters there, became virtuous. Saraswati river also participated in GAYA's yegeye and wa named VISĀLA, that came to Kurukshetra.

According to MAHABHARATA (VANA PARVA), on the inspiration of Maharishi NARAD, in reply to Yedhistra, sage PULSATEYE, stated the importance of pilgrimage, that after Puskar pilgrimage (the foremost) in Treta Yuga, Kurukshetra was important in DVAPRA yuga, but in KALI YAGA (the present age), the pilgrimage on the Ganges, gained importance as beneficiary. By a very dip in Puskar, Kurukshetra, Ganges or in Maagadh desh, one gains piety for his ancestors upto seven descents.

To gain fully from a pilgrimage, the essential qualifications of a person are:-

1. Whose hands are not impure in taking alms and by bad deeds.
2. Whose feet fall on earth by not trampling over living creatures but walk for benefit of others.
3. Whose mind is free from ill will towards others.
4. Whose knowledge is against violence and conflicts.
5. Whose worship is for self purity and for the welfare of the universe.
6. Whose deeds and actions are spotless.
7. Who does not accept charity from others and is content with whatever he gets.
8. Who is free form pride and ego.
9. Who is free from desires and power.
10. Who eats less and keeps his senses under control.
11. Who is free from all sins and evils.
12. Who does not become angry on others.

13. Who is truthful by his nature and behaviour.
14. Who considers the difficulties and worries of others, as his own.

By pilgrimage, one, even the most poor, gain successfully, as is obtainable by big yageyas (sacrifices). Such is the value of a pilgrimage to Kurukshetra, the region of Saraswati Goddess.

MORE HOLY PLACES

In addition to the sacred places, described in Chapter V, other places of importance are :-

ADITI TIRATHA: An ancient tirath spot, on the bank of river Saraswati, mentioned in MAHABHARATA IX Ch 49.17.

ADITI KUNDA: It is a dry pond to the east of the village Amina 5 miles from Kurukshetra, once the hermitage of the sage KASHYAPA and his consort Aditi. Near the hermitage is a temple of SIVA, which is beautified with two images of red stone (Kalyan Tirath Ank Jan 1952).

AGNI KUND: A holy place on the Saraswati (Vamana Purana 51-52).

AGNI TIRATHA: A holy spot on the bank of the Saraswati (Mahabharata IX Ch 47,13.14; Padma Purana 27.27).

ANYATAHPLAKSA: Name of a lotus lake in Kurukshetra, where king PURURAVAS was reunited with his beloved URVASI, after a long period of separation.

TEMPLES

In the late Chalukyan style, built about 1000 A.D., there is a group of temples at Gadag (Karnataka), dedicated to TRIKUTESWARA, Saraswati and Somesware. Temple of Saraswati (Goddess of learning and consort of B'rhma) is now in dilapidated condition, but still one can see the beautiful pillars of the mandappa. These pillars are in different patterns; ceilings and the doorways are remarkable for their exquisite carvings.

KANYAKUMARI TEMPLE:

Kanyakumari is celebrated for it shrine dedicated to Devi Paraśakti. The sea surrounding the temple contains many holy tiratha ghats like Sāvitri, Gāyatir, Saraswati, Kanyā, Sthanu, Mathur, Pithru etc.

HOYSALA STYLE TEMPLES:

A temples in Hassan District, at Basti Halli, of Hoysala style, dedicated to PĀRŚVANĀTHA, with fourteen polished black stone pillars, has a sculpture of a seated Saraswati in the Nvaranga. The VARDHAMANA basti at Santigatta (Bangalore district) has a temple of Hoysala kings geneology, where the image of Prabhāvati is about one meter high. Seated metallic images of padmāvati, Jvalāmalini, Saraswati, Panća Paramesthins, Nava Devatās are found in the temple.

PEHOWĀ TEMPLE

In the north at PEHOWĀ (Karnal-Harayana), the most important old temples are those of Saraswati, Kartikkeye and Mahādeva (Siva). The image in this small temple is of Saraswati, riding on a swan. It is made of Makrana stone marble.

Though no separate carrier vehicle for Saraswati, is mentioned; Hamsa or swan (goose), the vehicle of B'rhma, her spouse, is usually associated with the Goddess Saraswati also.

In popular mythological literature and pictures, a peacock is also shown as her carrier vehicle.

SARASWATI

CHAPTER XIII
ICONOGRAPHY, SCULPTURE AND PAINTINGS

Since Prehistoric times, images of Mother Goddesses have been made and the artists have exhibited their skill in sculptures and paintings of different Goddesses.

The Female divinity of ŚAKTI in Indian religion and art, symbolises form, energy or manifestation of the human spirit in all its rich and exuberant variety. The images of female divinities are far more diverse than those of Viṣnu, Śiva or to Boddhisatvas. The icons of the mother deity range form the benignant brooding motherliness of Pārvati, the screen dignity of Prajnaparāmitra and Saraswati or the nubile charm of UMĀ to the omnipotence and majesty of Durgā slaying the demons and the weird vigour of the dancing and grinning Camunda and Kāli wearing the garland of skulls.

In art, Goddess Saraswati is represented as a graceful woman with white complexion, wearing a crescent moon on her brow, riding a swan or a peacock or is seated on a lotus flower. Pure white swan. as the carrier of Goddess Saraswati (Gāyatri) indicates that to invoke her, the devotee should make his 'inner self' as pure as a swan. It is said that the swan has the power of discrimination between the right and the wrong; pure and impure, so the swan only picks up pearls from the sea and not the insects.

In an ivory statue, preserved at Obsterreichische National Bibliothek, Vienna; Saraswati (Goddess of poetry and music) stands on a lotus, accompanied by her vehicle the swan. She holds a veens (musical string instrument) in her two hunds, a book in the third and a lotus twine in the fourth.

Griffith, with reference to ATHARVA VEDA (4,20.7) mentions an uncommon variety of a image of MATSYA (Visnu incarnation) with four armed Visnu, flanked by Laksmi and Saraswati, each placed on a small lotus springing from the main lotus stalk. The image is at Bajrayogini (Bengal), as referred by R.S. Banerjee. Since primordial times, Saraswati has been a reverred deity in Brahaminism, Buddhism and Jainism. She is the founder Goddess of knowledge, science and arts. She is remembered by many names. In Buddhist literature, her chief names are MAHĀ SARASWATI, Arya Bajar Saraswati, Bajar Veena Saraswati, Bajar Sharada etc. In TANTRIC Buddhism, she is recognised as equivalent to MANJUSHBRI, PRAGYA, PARMITA, in the performance of education, memory and transmission of knowledge.

In Jainism, Saraswati Goddess also has a very high prestigious status in reverence. In Hinduism, she is worshipped as BāgDevi, Sharda and Veenā Bādini.

According to the PURANAS, the origin of Saraswati Goddess was from the mind of B'rhma, as a psyche daughter. She is the Sakti of B'rhma and that is why she is shown as the consort of B'rhma in Indian art and literature. All her material ingredients are radiant shining, spotless white garments, white lotus throne and white swan conveyance.

ICONOGRAPHY, SCULPTURE AND PAINTINGS

PAINTING

During the period, 1,000 AD to 1300 Ad, amongst the Goddesses, AMBIKĀ, Saraswati or Vāg Devi, Cakreswari and Padmāvati, were commonly worshipped.

In HADOTI region, at BUNDI, also called 'CHHOTI KASHI', because of many temples as in Kaśi, but also because of traditional pilgrimage by Sanskrit and Hindi scholars to pay special reverence to Bāg Devi. In Chhoti Kaśi, on account af art loving rulers, different manifestation of Bāg Devi Saraswati have been drawn in sketches and paintings. Not only in and outside the temples, but also in step wells, tanks and cenotaphs, different images of Goddess, in many forms have been produced.

In the world famous 'CHITRŚĀLĀ' (art gallery), attractive artistic drawing of Saraswati can be seen. These are based on the PURĀNAS, Silpasāstra, Pratimā Vigyan and Chitrasutra literary classic works, a reference to which has been given in 'ROOP MANDAN and 'MĀNSĀR'.

Saraswati miniature, reproduced in this book (Plate) is the precursor of the characteristic Jaina style, which thereafter dominated manuscript illustration (JNATA SUTRA). The projecting further eye is absent, in the miniature.

SCULPTURE:

In Aśutosh Museum, Calcutta, there is a twelvth century carving of VEENA VĀDINI. In the temples in South India, at HELEBID Bellur, there is an image of Saraswati Goddess. In the PRINCE of Wales museum, Bombay, there are selected images of Saraswati, of the medieval period. One image of BĀG DEVI SARASWATI, adores the British museum in London (UK). Thus Saraswati's grace is spread far and wide in different countries.

The two Saraswati images discovered in PALLU (Bikaner) match any image in carving and beauty as seen in different museums. One of these images was sent to London for display in Indian galery in 1948. It was a great attraction for the spectatores and a matter of discussion among art critics. Then it was sent to USA. On its return of India, it became a permanent artifact in National Museum, New Delhi. This image is made up from Makrana marble; standing on an blossomed lotus on a brightly coloured throne, in a peaceful posture, Saraswati is looking at her onlooker devotees. The second image, now in Government Museum, Bikaner, has a beautiful elegance, in the upper part is JINESWARA Bhagwan and near the shoulders of the Goddess Saraswati, are the gods welcoming her. The whole is decorated with deities, men, devotees, lotus flowers etc. The formation of the Goddess reflects the flow of limitless source of knowledge.

The craftsmanship in the two images in similar and the work of an expert sculptor. Carving many image in one and the same stone, is a job, which only an expert master can do. After seeing this image, Dr Stella Kramrisch, an authority on Indian art, said,' It is an extraordinary piece of examplary sculpture on such a big stone, so beautiful and emotional face expression, with fineness of ornaments and tenderness in the upper part.' Dr Goetz compared this work with the technique of sculpture in Gujerat because Solanki Kaumar Pal (1143-1172) favoured Jainism. During his reign, Jain traders spread this art to different parts of India. Now, this is attributable to Rajasthani sculptors, who were well versed with Jainism religion and culture. Dr Goetz, on its technique opines:.' Th perfection in the parts of the body, proportionate, exquisiteness, normal posture and the fineness of the ornaments, exhibits the perfect expertise of the craftsman.'

JAINA SCULPTURES

Some excellent specimens of India art of the age, like from the Bikaner region and the ornamental torana at Osia, were the creations of Jain sculptors. They display precision of details and associated ornamentation to the required degree. The Bikaner Bāgdevi in marble bears a remarkable placidity of expression. JAIN SARASWATI, by herself, does not hold a veena in her hands. The four armed, milk white image holds a white lotus in upper right hand, a book in the left, a rosary in the lower right and a coomandal (waterpot) in the lower left hand. Her hair style is moderately apical. Except the nostrils, the whole body is almost decorated with ornaments. On either side of the image are the images of women playing on Venna. Some images of the devotees and donors have also been carved around the main image. From artistic point of view, it looks as if the chisel of the sculptor was under the hand of the Goddess Saraswati herself.

In the form, circular, angular turn of the hands and feet are all in rhythmic movements. The slender body and sharp features show the expertise of the sculptor and his appreciation of the beauty in women. Makrana white marble has been rightly selected. Smaller figures have been so carved, that their presence enhances the beauty of the main image.

In the collection in Lucknow museum, there is one Jaina Saraswati obtained from Mathura, belonging to KUSAN period.

The Mahant Ghasidas memorial museum at RAIPUR, has a much damaged red stone sculpture of Saraswati (ht 79 Cm), which represents the four handed VIDYĀDEVI seated in Lalitāsana. Her head and hands are broken, but a Veena held in her lower right and left hands is visible.

SARASWATI IMAGE IN NATIONAL MUSEUM

This image, originally from Pallu (Bikaner), referred earlier, is a 1.48 meter hight image, in white marble, which shows the Goddess Saraswati standing gracefully in Tribhanga pose on a full blown lotus and holding in her various hands a rosary, a white lotus, a palm leaf manuscript tied with a silken string and a water vessel. She wears an elaborate tiara and other ornaments, a diaphanous sari, secured with an elaborate girdle, with its pearled tessels and festoons falling on her thighs. On either side she is flanked by female attendants playing on the Veena, held in their hands. Behind the head, near the lotus halo, appears the miniature image of TIRATHANKARA. The donor and his wife appear on the pedestal on the left and the right sides. A swan (the carrier of the Devi) appears on the pedestal in front. The image reflects the high water mark of Cahamana art of the 12th century AD.

PRAYER

'Let the Divine Saraswati, who is as fair as the garland of moon rays, who is clad in white garments, who is carrying a Veena (lute) in her hands (whose hands look

ICONOGRAPHY, SCULPTURE AND PAINTINGS

beautiful bearing the Veena gracefully), who is setting on a white lotus, who is always prayed to by Gods led by B'rhma, Visnu and Mahes and who destroys all lethargy; May she protect Us'. Being fond of white, she is as pure and unblemished as the white colour. By worshipping her, we acquire peace. She is worshipped by all Gods; as she is an authority, not only of academic learning, but also of fine arts, like music and dance. She uses a peacock or a white swan as her carrier, a fan as emblem of fine arts. Saraswati makes human beings, thoughtful, and rids and mind of all lethargy. Her worship makes one modest, ever ready to fight injustice and a belief in equality, fraternity and freedom.

INTELLIGENCE, WISDOM AND KNOWLEDGE are her boons." SHRI HAVIN SARASWATI SWAHA'.

SARASWATI MANTRAS

'ON YEY(N) HEE(N) SRI KALI SARASWATEY BUDDHJANANEYE SWAHA'.

'OM SRI HEE(N) SARASWATEYE NAMO'.